Poems by Dales Children

Twenty Years of Verse
from Askrigg Primary School, Wensleydale,

collected and compiled
by

Isabelle McGregor

Illustrations by
Fred Lawson and Muriel Metcalfe

DALESMAN BOOKS
1977

THE DALESMAN PUBLISHING COMPANY LTD.,
CLAPHAM (Via Lancaster), NORTH YORKSHIRE

First Published 1977

ISBN: O 85206 430 6

Isabelle McGregor and the Dalesman Publishing Company gratefully acknowledge financial support from the Yorkshire Arts Association towards the publication costs of this book. Any profit to the compiler from its sale will be used at her discretion to assist youth work in the area of the Askrigg Primary School.

Printed in Great Britain by
GEO. TODD & SON,
Marlborough Street, Whitehaven.

CONTENTS

Front cover and drawings on pages 9, 15, 20, 41, 51 and 60 by Muriel Metcalfe. Other illustrations by Fred Lawson.

ACKNOWLEDGMENTS

TO publish even a modest book of this nature calls for the co-operation of many people, and this has been very generously given to me. Therefore I wish to express my gratitude to the managers of Askrigg Church of England Primary School, under their chairman, the Rev. Malcolm Stonestreet, and to the North Yorkshire Education Authority for their permission to publish work done in their school, as I do to the numerous writers who responded so readily to my requests.

I should also like to thank for their encouragement Mr. J. Jordan, the North Yorkshire Educational Adviser, and Mr. R. B. Chalmers, Her Majesty's Inspector of Schools, as well as the poet and former H.M.I., Leonard Clark, who was kind enough to read my work, of which this book only represents a small part, at an early stage. For much initial advice and interest I am very grateful to Miss Julia MacRae and to the author, William Mayne.

My gratitude is extended particularly to Mr. Michael Dawson and the Yorkshire Arts Association for their valuable assistance with publication, and for their belief in the worth of the book. Finally, I wish to express my deep appreciation to Muriel Metcalfe for allowing some of the drawings of her late husband, Fred Lawson, as well as some of her own, to be used in illustration.

FOREWORD

IT was my good fortune in childhood to be taught to read by the time that I was four years old, and before that I had been firmly clutching a stout blue pencil to make my mark on whatever paper came my way. Though I knew nothing then of the alphabet and its magic I had been writing in my own way, and that was the important thing, as such experiences are for all children. The memory of the enjoyment thus gained never left me, and I believe that, subconsciously, it has always influenced my work with children.

My schooldays and many of my teaching years were to pass during a period of more or less stringent economy, but from the moment that I took charge of a school—my first and only one, as it came about—I was determined that, come what might, besides the great variety of books that I intended to amass for the children, paper and pencils in plenty would always be available for them, so that they could try out their ideas, not once, but over and over again, if they wished, until they were satisfied. I believed that all children had a great deal to say, and that, given every opportunity they would say it, sometimes forcefully, frequently with conviction, nearly always attractively. Throughout the years this belief became even firmer, and I continued to be rewarded by reading piece after piece of good, thoughtful, creative work. However badly written or mis-spelled at times, the intention, the ideas, the ability were there.

The best of the stories, the poems, the little pieces, I stored at first like any squirrel; they were pasted in booklets or mounted on the walls and generally enjoyed. Any effort was worth while to encourage this work, and parents and visitors often read it with pleasure. The day came, however, when, fearing to become too much of a hoarder, I began to give it away, sometimes even to throw it away, and much was lost that was of real interest. Finally, it was only some of the poems that I was keeping, as each summer came round, simply for my own enjoyment in after years; and even then, if a child expressed a wish for a particular booklet he would be given it, so how much has been lost that was worth saving I shall never know. I did know that what I kept would give me pleasure when some day I should read it again—and it does. When I pause to reflect that work of this kind is not unique, but that it is being done in schools everywhere, I wonder how many attempts of real value to mankind have disappeared almost as soon as they were written down.

There is, to my mind, about this verse a quality, a warmth, a sensitivity, often a turn of phrase, sometimes a humour, a sympathy, occasionally a philosophy, that should be shared, and as one follows

through the work of particular children, it is seen that style develops, too. If I had continued simply to store these rather musty books and grubby, dog-eared scraps of paper, few would have known the thoughts that so many children of eight or ten have been able to write down; so, almost at the end of twenty-two years, and with retirement very close, I came to feel that an attempt should be made to publish some of the most interesting poems, particularly some of those reflecting the local scene, and in this project I have been greatly encouraged by the few people whom I have consulted.

Let me, briefly, try to describe the environment of the children, so that the reader can, to some extent, share the perspective of the young writers. Askrigg stands, bleakly yet beautifully, high in Wensleydale, thought by many to be Yorkshire's loveliest dale. Diminished in size and population since there were lead miners and knitters and workers in wool and flax and corn grinding in its little mills, the village has the aspect of a small town, with an air, which has lost nothing with the years, of robust independence and purpose. Two of its men went to London to receive its market charter in the year before the Armada sailed. There was a school here in the eighteenth century, and the present one, rugged and grey, stone built and strong, and typical of many of the period, dates from 1877. Perched on a Pennine hillside, the school catches all the winds in their many moods. The scaurs and moors stand high above; the river Ure (here often known as Yore) in the valley below, the village street with its many Georgian houses, the church and the market cross, now only a reminder of the buying and selling that once went on in the square, are all close by. Within a mile or two are several little hamlets of which Askrigg is the focal point. Newbiggin, Nappa Scar, Woodhall, Bowbridge and Skellgill are all names that conjure up a picture of the countryside.

In the then two class primary school, the number of children climbed each summer to the high or middle fifties, and fell a little in the autumn. In 1963 the numbers were augmented by the children who were transferred from the neighbouring village of Carperby, four miles away, when its school was closed. Many families have had their roots here for at least three centuries, and these are they whose lives are largely concerned with the land. There are some family names that will often be seen to recur. There is a variety of occupations among the parents: shopkeeper and mechanic, lorry driver and teacher, vicar and carpenter, road worker and builder, electrician and clerk, plumber and accountant, postman and farmer, coal merchant and butcher. There was then considerable stability of population; any real transience always seemed to be slight, negligible in some years, greater in others when perhaps as one family or two moved out another moved in. Most people who came here tended to remain, but the pattern is beginning to change.

In a district such as this the weather has a considerable influence over our lives, and never goes un-noticed. It can provide either an excuse or a challenge, and has played no small part in forming the dalesman's character. Winters can be hard and long: the rain, the wind, the snow and the frost have to be battled against. The advent of spring, with the lambs, the swallows and the primroses, brings a gentle joy. Hot days in summer still mean late nights in the hayfield, even though the quiet, rhythmic raking of other years has long given place to the feverish carrying of bales. Summer holidays sometimes mean a visit to the sea, but it is not everyone who takes an annual holiday. The excitement of bright autumn tints and high winds, of fruits and thistledown, of gales and floods leads on to Christmas with its gaiety. And interspersed in the year-long catalogue are parties and Sunday School trips, Church and Chapel and the life that revolves round them, Guy Fawkes' Day and football matches, school games and Sports Day, music festivals and swimming expeditions. The school day brings its own diversions and excitements as well as its difficulties, and always, whatever the day or the time of year, there are fresh people, old stories and new ideas to capture the imagination.

That is the background of this book. Nothing was forced. I never asked the children to pick up their pencils to do this work unless the moment and the mood were right. These lines have all been done in school, quite spontaneously, some in a remarkably short time, but always in one day, and I know that they are genuinely the children's own work. Some wrote a poem while others wrote pages—or just a very few lines—of prose, and some made a picture. Afterwards it was usually necessary for spelling to be corrected, and a fair copy made, but both the many oddities and also the frequently surprising correctness of the punctuation are the children's own. To me, the really exciting thing is that these poems were all done, over a period of more than twenty years, by children aged from about eight to eleven, in this one school, this one class, with the one teacher. The school enjoyed a long period of stability, both home and school environments were fairly constant, and the teacher was as constant as I could make her. Experiences widened somewhat with the years, both in and out of school, but change did not hurry, and the beauty and character of the countryside have remained. We had the stimulus of a good library and later the occasional, chosen television broadcast to portray more dramatically other places, other people, other times, as well as important current events. And always I tried to encourage the children to listen, to look, to feel and to imagine.

The verse chosen for this volume is very largely about the countryside, and there is no great concern with the outside world. The children who wrote the verses were young—none of them more than eleven—and they were reflecting the life—the rural life—that they knew. Fortunately for most of them, they had not become little adults; they had not been rushed through the barriers into the bewildering, urgent world where life with all its problems and complexities was waiting. Their life was, and largely still is, made up of home and school; play, pets and bicycles; flowers and birds; swimming and gardening; Cubs, Brownies, Guides; helping on the farm or in the house, and watching the favourite television programme of the moment. It may be that in the country we barricade ourselves too firmly inside our ivory towers, but who are we to force on young children an awareness of the world they have not yet met, which is, all too surely, just round the corner? For the most part, death and divorce, debt and drink have not been encountered, and there has been no need to bring the door-key to school. Very rarely have disaster and delinquency impinged. In the surroundings that the children have known, happiness and security are reflected, and a growing maturity is apparent.

At the end, it may be asked: "Was this work worth saving?" In the last analysis the book may be difficult to judge, and it will be impossible to make comparisons. It must be taken for what it is: a collection of thoughts and observations on the life experienced by a long procession of country children before they left the primary school, and their efforts to express it in a particular form of words. About my own answer to the question I am confident.

What poetry, it may be asked, did the children hear? From five years old, in an infants' class which also had remarkable stability, with one enthusiastic teacher remaining for fifteen years, they were nurtured on the nursery rhymes and any well written poetry that they could enjoy. Always, at every stage, there was read to the children, as the years went by, a very great variety of good poetry—ballad, narrative, nature, nonsense: a great deal of Walter de la Mare, W. H. Davies and Robert Bridges, some Browning and Masefield, Wordsworth and Robert Frost, Edward Lear, Kipling and John Clare, the occasional poem of Drinkwater, Eliot, Keats and Auden, some Blake and Shakespeare—anything I thought they could understand and gain pleasure from hearing.

It will be noticed, of course, that among the poems in this collection there are numerous pieces with the same title, but if they had been written with even the slightest idea of publication something might have been done about it at the time. As it was, the title rarely seemed to matter much. "Truth is the hiyest thing that Man may kepe", wrote Chaucer, and in this spirit the children largely did their work. They always knew that they could write exactly what they liked, but it must be sincere—it must be "their own".

Many of these verses will be read and enjoyed by other children, though it was not the work of their contemporaries on which I nourished my writers: I believe the occasional taste of other children's efforts is enough for them. I think that the anthology's strongest appeal will, and should, be to adults, for whom it will mirror the minds of the very young, through the comments that they make, and will thereby lead to a closer awareness of the sometimes lowly beginnings of poetry, and of its great importance to children. The planning of this book is a task that I have greatly enjoyed, and it is my hope that this volume will bring its readers the same delight that compiling it has given me.

— Isabelle McGregor.

October, 1977.

muriel metcalfe

1: SNOW AND ICE

IN a Yorkshire dale there are few winters without at least one fairly heavy snowfall. It may not always last long, but even if the thaw comes quickly, snow never fails in its power to delight children. In some winters, such as those I particularly remember—1955, 1963, late 1965 and 1966—when snowstorms were very severe and prolonged, school life was sharply affected, if not disrupted, often for several days together. Many of the children had to travel some distance by school bus, and occasionally there would be a morning when an overnight snowfall had drifted heavily in a strong wind, and roads would be blocked before dawn. Then the bus could not run, and the only children at school would be those living in the village and those within a mile or so, who were nearly always possessed of sufficient determination to manage to walk. At such times the classes would be much reduced in numbers, but both work and play would go on with an added zest. It was, indeed, in a school where much of our progress was by means of individual work, days like these that emphasised the advantages of small classes, for teachers and pupils alike.

Apart from slides and snowballs and building igloos, and generally revelling in the fun of winter, children were well aware of the often serious problems caused by snow: the delayed transport of milk, the search for sheep overblown on the high ground when a storm came with little warning; the failure of buses to arrive; the extra work that had to be done by the roadmen with snowplough and shovel, and indeed by the school caretaker. Once we watched the comings and goings of a helicopter as it dropped bundles of hay and supplies at a temporarily isolated farm a mile or two away.

Snow always provided us with ideas for work, of course. The shapes of animals' footprints, the lengths of icicles, the ice on the pond in the school garden and the hexagonal pattern of the snowflakes all served as inspiration. Lovely pictures, too, were produced, and I remember how impressive the winter scene could look in chalk and charcoal.

I think the number and variety of the poems about winter, each charming in its own way, shows its dominance in the minds of the children. One, by an eight year old boy, has already been published by Paul Jennings in The Living Village, compiled from a study of scrapbooks made by Women's Institutes in 1965, their Golden Jubilee year. He found it in the winning entry for Yorkshire, done by Askrigg W.I., and this poem was contributed by the school.

Winter Time

In winter time the fire glows red,
The birds on table scratch for bread,
The foxes' prints show bold and clear,
The rabbits' tracks go far and near.

The snowdrops start to push up through
The rock-hard snow, a whitey-blue,
The river's frozen up with ice,
The cellar shelters two dear mice.

The housewife's brewing up the tea
After scrubbing the floor, on knee,
The sheep are eating musty hay,
The postman goes along his way.

The oak tree starts to bud afresh,
Stoats squeeze through some wire mesh,
The otter smiles a wicked sneer,
They wish you all a Happy New Year.

David Hodgson (11).

Snowflakes

One morning when I looked,
It was snowing.
Snowflakes came down
To the ground.
With its soft cold feel,
It goes crunch under your feet.
Snowballs go whizzing past.

Nicholas Addinall (9).

Snow falling softly
Far on the distant hill-tops,
A blanket of white.

Lynn Newton (11).

Snow

It snowed a lot in '47,
It seemed to come right down from heaven.
We fight with snow,
And soon the foe
Cries, 'Mercy! Woe!'

Our enemy is in a plight,
So it soon takes to hurried flight.
No longer are we flinging snow,
To and fro, to and fro,
Oh, no, no, no, oh, no!

We pursue the fleeing girls,
Once again the snowball whirls.
I hit Vivian on the head,
And gave Nina a snowy bed,
When she got up I think she fled.

Peter Chevins (9).

Winter

Winter has come at last,
And the snowflakes are whirling fast.
The snowballs are whirling through the air,
And everything is quite bare.

With our sledges off we scurry,
Down the hills in such a hurry,
Skating on the frozen lakes,
And then go home to eat hot cakes.

Susan Banks (10).

Winter Time

When the Winter time is here
Everything from far and near
Is as white as white can be,
And an icicle hangs from
A small boy's bicycle.
And when it snows,
And the wind blows,
We get drifts.

Richard Brisbane (8).

Winter at Night

At night in winter,
It is very bitter, and icicles hang
On the edges of roofs.
Every hour they grow
Inch by inch by inch,
And they grow bigger and bigger
And bigger.

Ian Percival (9).

Fun in the Snow

When the snow falls on the ground,
Everything glistens around,
It falls on fields and flowers and trees,
And goes wherever it does please.

Children playing here and there
Laugh with happiness, and not a care
Have they; they love the snow,
And play in it wherever they go.

Oh, look! A snowman over there,
He's even sitting on a snow chair,
He's got grit in his head,
And a scarf of vivid red.

Rebecca Gitlin (10).

The Cold Days

When icicles hang on the roof,
And snow clings to the sheep's hoof,
The time when rats are thin
From want of food from the farmer's bin.

When Rabbits and Hares lie dead,
Partly because the snow on their feet is as heavy as lead;
The time when food is scarce for the birds,
And the bullocks are gathered in herds.

When moles will burrow at the top of the ground,
And snowflakes madly whirl around,
In a month or two spring comes again,
And the rats get fat from the farmer's grain.

Frank Fawcett (10).

A Winter Frost

In the snow the children fall,
All the icicles hang on the wall.
And all at once the wind will blow
A cloud of cold white snow.
When they are cold and wet, home they go,
And take off their wellingtons which are full of snow.
When they come home with noses red,
It soon is time to go to bed.
In the morning up they get,
Early are out and soon are wet.

Pamela Metcalfe (11).

Walking in the Snow

Walking up the snowy hill,
Walking past the frozen mill,
Walking in the snowy morning,
Walking when the day is dawning.

Walking into land unknown,
Walking in the Arctic zone,
Walking in the snowy morning,
Walking when the day is dawning.

Walking in the whitest lands,
Walking on with frozen hands,
Walking in the snowy morning,
Walking when the day is dawning.

Andrew Brisbane (10).

Snow

One winter day when
Icicles hung from walls
And snow blew all ways
And sheep in the fields nearly
Covered with snow
And snow shone silver outside
And house tops covered with
The glittering snow
And the milk man rushed
To and fro with the milk,
Children went running
With their sledges
Through the field.
The people in their
House by the fires
And little children
Brought in logs
For their fire.

Alan Cooper (9).

Snow on the hill tops
Cold and glinting in the sun,
Finally melting.

Pat Metcalfe (11).

March Morning

It was a cold and snowy day,
All the children were out at play.
Most were sledging down the hill,
Which is near an old, old mill.
All the puddles along the lanes are frozen.
When the sun comes out to thaw the snow,
All the ice on the puddles will go.
The icicles begin to fall,
Until there are none left at all.
Everything is beginning to thaw,
And of the snow there is no more.

William Banks (11).

2: FLOWERS

FLOWERS, especially the wild ones, always occupied a large and important part of school time. We were ideally situated to find growing a wide variety of plants, ranging from those of the high pastures on the limestone down to those in the low-lying fields of the river valley. There were, too, always a few children who knew where to look for the rare flowers that they must, on no account, gather, and there was one of these that we carefully watched over in the school garden.

Early in the year we started our flower table, with snowdrop and celandine, coltsfoot and daisy, dandelion and dog's mercury, primrose and wood anemone following each other, and then a swift succession crowding in, the white and the yellow being followed by the blue and the pink and the purple, as the year moved onward. So that the children could become familiar with the names of as many wild flowers as possible each year, a great attempt was made to ensure that they were really aware of what flowers were growing and learned to recognise them. Throughout the winter we had a succession of bulbs growing in bowls—crocuses, hyacinths, tulips and daffodils—which gave us colour and beauty on the dark days and always a sense of new life arising from the old. We never had a dead time in school.

From a former day, when there had been senior boys of up to fourteen and over, I had inherited a large and wild garden, which I was nevertheless, determined to use, because I realised that it could provide young children with worthwhile experience. In the first year or two my father came and pruned the bushes and I planned the garden afresh. It was not long before our work was being rewarded, and for the whole of my twenty-two years it was not only a source of joy to me but a hive of activity and discovery for the children. I remember, for example, how surprised they were, when my mother bought us our first roses, to learn that each bush had its own particular name.

The daffodils which had grown in school each winter were planted outside in the autumn, year by year to increase the display of spring colour out of doors, along with the forget-me-nots and wallflowers. Opening, as the garden did, from the playground, we had the benefit of its colour by day, and eventually we managed to have a lovely succession of flowers throughout the year. In the milder autumns we were often able to bring in the last of the roses, usually the fragrant Iceberg, to mix with the holly at Christmas. We grew a varied supply of vegetables, most of which the children took home, and others were eaten for school dinners, "School" cabbage and "School" lettuce being thought infinitely superior to anything bought from shops. The children did all the work themselves, the bigger boys doing the digging, a little at a time, and as the months went by they enjoyed seeing, and eating, the fruits of their labours.

So it was, to return to flowers, that of both the cultivated and the wild, so many were known. One year, I remember, we played our part in the production of a new Botanical Atlas of the British Isles, by carefully noting all the many flowers we could find in the particular grid of the Ordnance Map that was allocated to us. Year by year, especially in the prolific summer months, many were the hours, mostly at playtime and dinner-time, when children would pore over our large number of wild flower books to try and identify an elusive specimen. In this pursuit, as in other ways, I have noticed so often the strength of the home influence. When a mother, or perhaps a grandmother, was interested in wild flowers, that interest was reflected over and over again in the children, to their lasting advantage.

This tiny handful of poems, then, about common well-loved flowers, helps to recall time well spent, either tending plants or learning to recognise them.

The Daisies in the Meadows

The daisies in the meadows,
Swaying in the breeze,
With little dainty petals,
With pretty golden centres,
They're rocking in the wind,
And waving in the breeze.

Ann Stirling (9).

Primroses

Primroses sway in the wind,
With green leaves and golden petals.
Children pick them in the Spring.

In my garden grows
A little bunch of Primroses.
I water them when they are thirsty.

When my Primroses die
I wait until in Spring
They shoot up again.

Angela Alderson (11).

A Trip to the River

One summer's day in the river
I saw a lot of marigolds.
They gleamed so bright in the stream.
They blew back and forward
And to and fro in the wind.
The wind was fast and blew
The marigolds faster.

Keith Percival (10).

Flowers

The bluebell is a pretty flower,
It loves the sun, enjoys the shower.
It wakes at morn, in pleasant sun,
And goes to sleep when work is done.

The primrose in the wood it lives,
And to the bees its pollen gives.
Its flower is of a golden hue,
And in the morn it's bright with dew.

The stitchwort, frail and white,
Has a secret, friendly, light.
Its tiny flower quickly grows,
In, and close by, the hedgerows.

Judith Banks (10).

The Bluebells

They sway and sway about
Like a pendulum on a clock.
The wind blows hard
And the more they sway about.
But then someone
Is coming up the hill,
And in no time
They are in a vase in the house.
Now they cannot
Sway and sway about.

Tom Fawcett (11).

3: THIS AND THAT

ONCE A TERM, for a number of years, we produced a class magazine, an all-embracing volume that was packed with a great variety of material which included many stories and poems written quite spontaneously on themes which had suggested themselves to the children. These magazines would continue to circulate until they finally fell to pieces and found their way to the waste paper basket. They served not only to display a large amount of interesting work but they acted as the stimulus to enthusiastic effort. As they disintegrated the contents were usually lost, but poems such as these show the wide range of small and great things—"this and that"—on which a child will pause and reflect in his own way for a short time.

A Distant Star

If I look at the sky at night,
When all the stars are burning bright,
I have a vision of a distant star,
Which from the earth is very far.

Michael Bell (11).

England

Sitting on the ground, look at the world.
See the hills and the bridges and the fells.
Look round for miles.
See birds, trees, cows and dogs.
Sing a song and it will make us happier.
Do not mutter, it will make you sad and cry.

Nell Dinsdale (9).

I Wish

I wish I had seen the country,
To walk about the wood,
I wish I had been in the pastures,
Where the cows are chewing cud,
But living in the city,
You cannot see one wood.

Andrew Lomax (8).

When I'm in the Country

I have a wonderful feeling
When I am walking in the country.
The birds are singing,
The little stream rustles as it passes by,
The daisies begin to flower,
They look so nice against the green grass.
The little lambs are playing together,
They skip and jump.
The lambs look so gay in the bright sun.

Julie Porter (10).

The Night

I can hear the stream tinkling,
And soon the stars will be twinkling,
And the moon will be shining soon,
And the night will have crept up to us,
The moon will make the lake glint,
Just like a piece of flint.

Duane Percival (9).

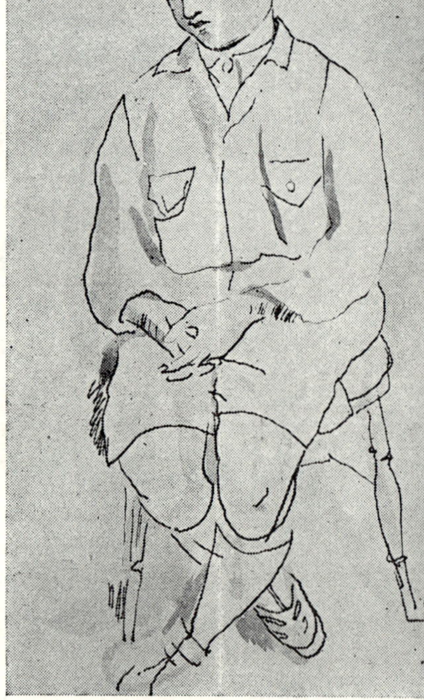

Space

Space is lasting on and on
In to Infinity,
Rockets have been to the moon
Several times,
But they have been nowhere else.
There might be some monsters
On their way to earth,
Maybe they have time machines,
Things that can get them
Anywhere.

Paul Corney (9).

Space

Up to the moon in a balloon,
Up to space,
Singing in bass,
Still in our balloon
We can now see the moon.
Let's get the bag
And stick in the flag,
When you're in space
It's a very nice place.

Shane Metcalfe (11).

The Aeroplane

Over the tree tops goes the aeroplane,
Over the mountains and forests and everywhere,
Looks on the lonely roads
And on the towns
Where people shop, here and there.

Mark Hammond (11).

Saturday Morning

On Saturday morning I play with my friend.
Or if he is not in,
I sometimes ride my bike.
I like to ride my bike on Saturday morning.
I like to go splashing through the pools of water.
It makes patterns and funny noises on the mud guard.
I sometimes have a ride on my friend's bike,
But that has no back mud guard on.
And if you go through any water
You get splashed all up your back.

David Alderson (11).

The Monkey

In the zoo there was a monkey,
And his name was little Jumpy.
He wore a hat trimmed with bows,
And little bells were on his toes.
He loved the little boys and girls,
Most of all the ones with curls.

Georgine Thwaite (10).

Bonfire Night

The sky was dark;
Tyres, boxes and pieces of wire
Were piled upon
The Bonfire.

The stars were
Twinkling in the sky,
The fireworks were
Shooting up high.

Children were Merry and Gay,
Shouting with joy,
Sparklers being held
By both girl and boy.

Elizabeth Weatherald (9).

The Sea

Deep, deep, down below, the fish come to and fro,
In between the coral they go,
Big fish, small fish, thin fish, fat fish,
Every shape and size.
They go in between old wrecks.
There is a shark coming,
There is panic! They swim for their lives.
They are safe now,
The shark has gone.
No one would have known he had been there.

Peter Gaskell (11).

The Mountain

When a man climbs the mountain
He can feel the cold icy wind at his face.
If they come to a crack
In the ground, a man might slip,
And they will have to pull him up.
The men leave heaps of stones,
So they will not forget
The way back.
When the men get to the top
There is a great joy inside them.

Stephen Crawford (10).

The Lost Farthing

I found a farthing on the shore.
It had a head and tail,
I think it was a 1900,
But I can't be sure.

A farthing was a half of a halfpenny
But it is no use now,
Because everything is so dear.
But this little Farthing was a special farthing
Because it was lost on the shore.

The tide was coming in very quickly
So I picked up my farthing and ran,
But, alas! I fell.
Away that farthing went
Rolling, rolling into the sea.

Mary Trotter (11).

The things that God made

God made the sky so blue,
God made the grass so green,
God made the water for our drink,
God made the flowers that smell so sweet
God made the sun that shines so bright.

Nina Cook (9).

The Weather

Drip, drip, drip,
Falls the steady rain.
Drip, drip, drip,
Down the window pane.

Flake by flake,
Ever so softly fall.
Flake by flake,
A tiny little ball.

Sunbeam by beam,
A golden light it gives.
Sunbeam by beam,
It lights us from our beds.

Breeze by breeze,
Blows about the clouds.
Breeze by breeze,
Blowing in the trees.

Judith Banks (10).

4: SPRINGTIME

ONE may think, at times, of the coming of spring with "the first mild day of March", and one is often mistaken, but when the change does come it is clearly seen. Suddenly, there is a fresh dimension in the children's play, and in their many activities. From this time they are noticing, and bringing with them to school, burgeoning catkins and bursting buds; they tell of the first appearance of hesitant wild flowers, the returning migrants, the first nests, the lambs. Outdoor games take on a new pattern; skipping ropes reappear, and the boys remember again the existence of forgotten cricket bats. It is no longer necessary to run about so vigorously in order to keep warm, and the little girls begin to play some of the traditional old singing games. Energy can be applied in fresh directions. There is a quickened tempo of life that continues through the busy summer, and an awareness in the children of this resurgence is apparent in these verses.

Spring and Winter

Winter has passed
And spring's here at last.
The lambs skip about
And the children shout.

The birds sing,
And the bells ring.
When the sun shines bright
It's a lovely sight.

Maureen Thwaite (10).

The Coming of Spring

The world has a refreshing air,
And joyfully frolics the mad March hare.
The trees are green, bees are seen,
For Spring is here.

The animals and birds arise
To view the beauty of the bright, Spring skies.
The dogs prance and children dance,
Summer is near.

Barbara Chapman (11).

Springtime

In Spring the birds begin to sing,
They fly so swiftly on the wing,
Stopping rarely for their rests,
They soon will be building their tiny nests.

The trees have all their new green leaves,
The sycamore with her small bunches of keys,
The rabbit hops to her burrow small,
Whilst the great oak lifts her branches tall.

In spring the little rabbits are born,
Frisking in and out the corn,
But the mother keeps a good look out,
To make sure the farmer isn't about.

Kathleen Trotter (11).

Spring

Spring is here,
The lambs kick,
The horses rear,
And sheep reach the sheep-lick.

The leaves are back,
And they get
The sun they lack
From last summer, when they met.

The flowers come out,
The birds twitter,
The children shout
And scatter litter.

Dean Cook (11).

O brilliant sun,
Shining down on the flowers
In the bright meadows.

Mary Fawcett (11).

Spring Time

In April time
When lambs are fine
The old crows call with an 'erk',
And the little lambs jump over
Their mother with a jerk.
The birds are making nests,
To the sheep they are pests.

Michael Alderson (10).

Spring Time

Spring is a season bright and gay,
Little lambs are here to play,
Over the hills and far away.
We may go as well to see
Little lambs who are happy.

Happy lambs at play
Over the hills and far away,
We may go as well to-day.
I have seen the little lambs
Still at play every day.

Angela Kirkbride (10).

Springtime

Spring is here, let us play,
Oh what fun we'll have to-day!
Listen to the birds singing,
And tiny buds are slowly springing.

The lambs are frisking to and fro,
Children skipping as they go,
The bees are humming round the hive,
And everything is coming alive.

With meadows green and flowers gay,
It is the merry month of May,
The rabbits hopping here and there,
There's lots of flies in the air.

A brisk wind begins to blow,
There is not a sign of snow.
Alas the Spring is soon gone,
It never lasts very long.

Margaret Humble (11).

5: BIRDS

WILD BIRDS and their song, their nests and eggs were every year a recurring source of interest. The coming of the curlew, the swallow and the cuckoo—so often heard but seldom seen—and the flight of the heron at the nearby stream, excitedly observed on the way to school, or the gulls at the tarn on the moor were all frequent and absorbing topics of conversation.

For a number of years all the junior children were members of the Royal Society for the Protection of Birds, and this connection was of enormous value. For the annual cost of just one old penny each, there was a gain in absorption of attitudes that was, I think, inestimable. Much time was devoted, year by year, to the study by each child of a different bird and also of a tree or flower. Careful records were kept, and it was of added value that so much of this work could only be done out of school, for it helped in directing the use of leisure time.

Country children take pleasure in watching the birds they see in field and garden, and this fondness for them, even when it does not appear to be accompanied by much factual knowledge, comes over clearly and warmly in these little verses.

The Robin

The night's been snowy
And the wind roared,
But still the robin comes singing at your door.
You think of the poor little thing,
Standing out in the cold alone,
So you put the poor thing some crumbs on the dust bin.

If another bird comes to the bin,
The robin will fight it and most likely win,
You would think the robin was a helpless thing,
But in winter it can still win,
You can feed it till it is full,
But it will still wait and hope for more.

Stephen Foster (10).

The Robin

I love the robin's little song
Chirruping, chirruping all day long,
His feathers are lovely, his breast is red,
You can see him clearly from far ahead.

He has a wife at home,
When he is left alone to roam.
I hope they will always stay with me,
In a nest beside my favourite tree.

They keep me company all the day
They never, never will go away.
He never seems to be full of sorrow,
His song seems to say 'I will come to-morrow'.

He comes when Christmas time is near,
His happy little song we hear.
He is a happy, gay little bird.
He sings the nicest song I have ever heard.

Rebecca Gitlin (10).

The bright feathered birds
Sitting on the tree above,
Singing so sweetly.

Margaret Gibson (11).

Birds

The blackbird has a lovely song,
He sings loudly all day long,
At night he goes to his big nest,
And crouches his head under his breast.

The robin has a red, red breast,
It makes a very tiny nest,
It lays five little pale blue eggs,
It perches on the clothes line pegs.

The owl she comes out during the night,
The barn owl, she is usually white.
She hoots and hoots, and wakes the bats,
And then goes hunting for the rats.

Michael Lambert (11).

Singing

The robin sings in winter,
The thrush sings in the spring,
The sky lark sings in summer,
And so does everything.

John Metcalfe (10).

The Kingfisher

The kingfisher sits nobly there,
A bird you would surely ken,
He awaits the chance a fish to catch,
He is surely the king of fishermen.

His family are waiting in a hole,
In the banking of a stream,
There is no British bird
Whose colours brighter gleam.

Ivan Johnson (11).

Birds

I like the robin,
When it's a-bobbing,
I like the thrush,
As he sings in the bush.

The big birds fly,
And the little birds cry.
In the sky you see the crows,
While the young one in the nest grows.

Jack Bell (10).

Friendly Birds

The robin, bluetit and the wren
Start tapping on the window pane;
And if you give them tit-bits
They're sure to come again.

The wren with stumpy little tail
Will eat the bread and nuts with glee,
It doesn't matter if they're stale,
He'll eat them up just for his tea.

The blue-tit with her bright blue cap
Will eat the fat strung on a line,
The corn spread out she'd rather leave
But coconut she thinks just fine.

The robin with his glossy breast
Will eat the corn and bread and all,
The coconut he will not leave,
He'll sing you to sleep with his call.

David Hodgson (11).

6: FLOWING WATER

THIS BOOK is largely filled with writing that is concerned with the facets of life that change so little and so slowly in the countryside. In a world of clamour, the hills and the streams are always about us, giving us at the same time both the serenity we need and also an awareness of the pulsating movement and the rhythm of nature. These are the constants, however much social customs may change, whatever new inventions may come to our aid or to complicate our lives.

These poems about rivers and streams—the "becks" of Yorkshire—all express similar thoughts. The children have listened to the water, watched it, sat by it, paddled in it, swum in it, and have sometimes looked on it with a feeling of awe. The bubbling, peaty brown streamlet of the heathery moorland, the ice-cold spring that forces its way through the limestone, the dark, still pool where the fishes jump, the waterfall that cascades steeply over the rocks, the lake, girdled by hills, from which a little river runs—the shortest river in England—and the larger river that is here still hurrying on its way; the floods that spread themselves in winter over the low-lying fields; the children know them all.

Water

The rippling water
Gleaming in the bright sunshine
All the long years round.

On a rainy day
Dark clouds float over our land,
Low in the grey sky.

Running down the hill
Water trickles down the beck,
In the bright sunshine.

Kathleen Smith (11).

The water flows by,
Over the rocky bottom,
By the still deep woods.

Susan Trotter (11).

Water

The river is in flood,
The stones are rolling down,
Nobody will go to the river to-day,
When the river is in flood.
The river is crashing, up against the rocks,
Little whirlpools here and there,
Big rushing waterfalls all over,
All the water going over the edge,
Knocking down some of the trees and walls,
Till lastly the flood calms down;
Then all is quite still and children come and swim.

Barbara Metcalfe (9).

Near the Stream

I heard the rumbling stones fall down the hill.
I heard the trickling stream run by,
I heard the birds screech in the sky,
I heard the eggs chip in the tree,
Did you hear anything like me?

Carol Cockerill (9).

The Stream

The stream flows merrily past the mill,
Standing, solitary, on the hill;
The stream never lingers night or day
But flows on faster all the way.

He sees the cows in the meadow there,
He sees the birds that fly in the air,
He waters the trees, the grass, the rushes,
He laughs and cries and never hushes.

He murmurs a song on his way to the sea,
'There's more than a mile between him and me'.
And when the sea comes into view
He says good-bye to me and you.

David Hodgson (11).

Water

Down the rocks it runs,
Gushing, gurgling, rushing, swirling on its way,
Slowly moving in the pools.
Pool after pool, going slowly, relaxing as it goes,
Reaching a water fall, falling over,
Hitting the bottom with a thundering splash,
People throwing stones, making it jump,
Playing with the fishes, making them hide,
Finally reaching its home, the sea.

Richard Allen (10).

7: BRIGHT SUMMER

WITH the arrival of the summer term the rhythm and pattern of life changed. Now the speeding weeks were filled with new calls for extra outbursts of energy. There was much to do, both at school and home, and there was great satisfaction in the doing. I think the poems in this section show the feeling of happy exuberance that abounded especially with the coming of the warmer and longer summer days.

In the early part of the term more concentrated work was done in the school garden for our season was very short. There was the fun of seeing radishes grow and potatoes pushing through the soil, of cutting a great variety of flowers; of watching, when the tulips faded, the brightness of Siberian wallflowers and the later glory of the "red hot poker". There was the race against the weeds and the quickly growing grass, and then, on some hot and sunny afternoon, the luxurious pleasure of sprawling on the neatly cut lawn at the bottom of the garden. Perhaps there is nowhere in life better than in a garden for learning the need for regular and continuing effort, and perhaps there are not many kinds of work that are more rewarding to the spirit. I think that some of the children, young as they were, unconsciously absorbed this truth. In their final year at school, when they were capable of doing the work best, they also learned that the crop from the seeds they sowed would have to be harvested by others.

From April onwards, more time could be spent on athletics in readiness for the sports, in running, jumping, skipping; and the relay races were fine examples of the effort that children will make to work together. At the same time, additional practice and polish were being given to music for the summer festival, when we travelled down the dale to join with other schools who all played their own part in a performance of surprising variety.

From 1970 examinations were no longer the deciding factor in the matter of a child's future destination, but the eleven year olds were all leaving, and a certain inevitable and essential reorientation always became apparent. A day was often spent visiting the new school, and from this time the children, like Janus, were looking both ways, at the little world they were leaving, and forward, too, with confidence and eager anticipation, to the new and larger world they were about to join—which is the way it should be.

The term always culminated in Open Day, when children, particularly the youngest, gained as much pleasure as their parents from seeing their work displayed and new skills demonstrated. All had something in which to take pride. There would be books of all shapes and sizes, crammed with work. The walls would glow with vivid art —not always easily intelligible—paintings, friezes, collage, fabric printing; tables full of objects made of clay, plaster of paris, polystyrene or papier mache; felt toys and cushions, aprons and dirndl skirts. There were all kinds of mathematical projects, too. I remember one long multicoloured strip of card that reached from floor to ceiling: it showed the amount of rain that had fallen on Askrigg, month by month, over a period of three years. What an amount of work that represented! And what an amount of rain!

Out of school, in the children's life at home, there was the great release of body and spirit that summer brings: walks to the moor, to the river, picnics and outings, more daylight for play; bicycle rides, later bedtime. All this comes out in the poems, whether in 1951 or 1971. To-day, even though the younger brothers and sisters of the teenagers may have their transistors and their pop records, and more pocket money to spend on ever more sophisticated playthings, the main pattern of their life in this beautiful countryside remains, in essence, comparatively unchanged.

Bright Summer

The sparrow sings,
The daisies bow their heads
In silver rings.

The swallow skims,
The blackbird warbles
All her hymns.

The swift flies high,
The lark sings as she
Sweeps the sky.

David Hodgson (10).

On the Moor

Up on the moor
I hear the snipe,
One wink and it is out of sight.

Down a hill, there's a beck in sight.
Look in a dub,
A fish may jump out.

Mary Scarr (9).

Summer Time

A peaceful road, and a parked car,
Maybe a pony being ridden,
Some melting tar,
This is summer time.

Children fishing with their nets,
Catching a minnow or two,
Teenagers with their radio sets,
Maybe in the wood a cuckoo,
This is summer time.

Little birds looking for worms,
The sweet smell of hay,
Then the quietness returns.
In the hay me and my friend play.
This is summer time.

Michael Gaskell (10).

In Summer

In summer the birds sing
Every night,
And every morning
The flowers are bright.

The sun is hot,
And lovely too,
Everybody knows,
Like me and you.

Every day
The sun does shine,
Lovely, and bright,
Red like wine.

Judith Cooper (10).

Hay Time

Hay time is a busy time,
The tractor does its round.
Sometimes there is trouble
When the tractor goes aground.

Sometimes when I'm helping
I stack the hay up high,
And always when I'm raking
I hurt my foot and cry.

Penelope Lomax (10).

Woodland Summer

Tweet, tweet, tweet, the swallow calls.
The green caterpillar up the gooseberry crawls.
The cricket chirps 'neath the old oak tree,
And every creature is as happy as can be.

Bzzzzzzz the busy bees
Flit to and fro among the green-coated trees.
The thick cool forest shelters from the sun
The wild woodland creatures, every one.

Carolyn Weatherald (10).

Summer

Big fluffy white dog,
Sitting in the bright sunshine
On the soft, green grass.

The sun is shining
High, in the blue summer sky
While the clouds float by.

The fish in the pond
Swim in and out of the weeds
While birds softly sing.

The butterfly rests
On a bright yellow flower,
Swaying in the breeze.

The black horse gallops
Down the hill towards the lake
Where the grass is green.

Vivienne Mallinson (11).

Summer is here

The summer now is here,
And all of us filled with good cheer.
The hedgerows are fragrantly scented;
The flowers are often tormented
By bees.

The sky is blue and white,
Soft and dreamy are the clouds.
The meadows are full of good grass,
One sheet, a golden mass,
Of buttercups.

Judith Banks (11).

Summer

In the summer the Cuckoo goes,
The Swallow skims where the river flows,
The Swift flies high up in the sky,
The Wagtail wags his tail; Why?
Because it is the summer.

The Jackdaw caws at the Rook,
The Dipper dips in the brook.
The grass upon the fells is dry,
The hare runs by the wall; Why?
Because it is the summer.

The Corncrake glides through the hay,
The sun is hot at the noon of the day.
The temperature is soaring high,
The Chaffinch chirrups; Why?
Because it is the summer.

The Curlew calls to his mate,
'Hatch those eggs, dear, or we'll be late',
The whirring wings of the Starling nigh,
The roses bloom; Why?
Because it is the summer.

David Hodgson (11).

8: ANIMAL FRIENDS

THE wild life of the countryside was always of great interest to the children, and all were familiar with the animals on the farms. Sometimes an unexpected sight, such as the stiffened, velvet body of a mole just trapped, evoked wonder and sympathy, or the discovery of a wasps' nest bigger than a man's head caused excited speculation. Once there was the unusual event of being filmed by Independent Television while searching for crayfish in quiet, secret water said to have been their habitat for hundreds of years—an episode, incidentally, which led to the writing of a popular story book about us, as well as a continuing interest in crayfish.

Again and again, imagination would be stirred by reading to the children. *The Wind in the Willows,* for instance, never failed to fascinate group after group, as they listened intently to the escapades and joys and sorrows of the little animals.

Much affection was lavished on pets. Cats and dogs were in most homes, and during the lambing season a pet lamb would often be found in the kitchen of a farming family. The children had other creatures to care for, too: rabbits, white mice, hamsters, gerbils, budgerigars, tortoises or goldfish, and many were the life histories and stories that were written about them. From time to time a talk was given by some friendly officer of the R.S.P.C.A., and the leaflets he distributed were always avidly read and acted upon.

Many of these poems show keen observation and a sympathetic feeling for the creatures written about, and some knowledge of their ways.

The Lambs

Little lambs are jumping and playing
In the green meadow fields,
The mother sheep are lazily lying
And some are eating an everlasting meal.

At night the lambs have races,
To and fro, from wall to wall,
The mother sheep walks, with sturdy paces,
When she hears the farmer's call.

Catherine Middleton (11).

The Lamb

A little lamb romps round a field,
His mother stands in a corner.
The little lamb just does not know what to do,
He is bewildered when he comes to a pool,
He sees his reflection,
And jumps back two inches,
For he is frightened, and runs to his mother.

Nicholas Hill (10).

The Old Donkey

An old neglected donkey stands
In a corner on his own.
I wonder what he's thinking,
He looks so sad and lonely.
He's very thin, I think I'll feed him.
It won't do any harm.
I give him a peppermint,
And what a noise he makes,
With his big yellow teeth,
Crunch, crunch, crunch.

Debra Tate (10).

The Frog

I saw a frog with a greeny-brown back,
And his round little tub was white.
A good name for him would be Jumping Jack!
In his eyes there twinkled a light.

His big black legs were very, very long,
While his little front legs were short!
Jumping Jack could sing a very croaky song,
It might be an octave short!

Simon Hodgson (11).

The Horse

The horse stands by the silver stream,
He puts his head down
And takes a long cool drink of water.
Then he listens to the water
Rippling over the stones,
And then puts up his head
And neighs and gallops off.

Ian Bell (9).

My Dog

My dog is such a large dog,
A lovely golden brown,
He eats his food with eagerness,
And sleeps from eve to dawn.

He takes me for a walk,
He scampers round about,
And waits for me to tie his lead,
Then take him, running, out.

Joan Chapman (11).

My Dog

My dog is called Rex,
He has a black coat,
He sleeps by the fire,
While we watch the T.V.

He is a Labrador,
And barks at the door
Whenever he wants to be in
Or out.

When he wants a drink
He jumps at the sink,
And barks and barks
Till we get him one.

John Banks (11).

The Mole

The mole is in his black coat.
He's going into his hole so deep.
He's hard at work digging a hole.
He's digging deep for a place to sleep.
He finds the end of his hole.
In a garden a trap shall be laid
And he shall be slayed in the green garden.
But he escapes down his hole of darkness.
He crawls back to the field and out of his hole.

Trevor Hammond (9).

Animals at Night

One sunny morning as the sun rose from the hills,
Big animals walked proudly through the wood,
But small animals beware of the dangerous animals,
Taking short, quick runs to hide behind the tufts of grass.

Owls, hooting in the night up in this tall, dark tree,
Badgers, growling in the hollows of the ground,
Mice, squeaking as they run through the tall tufts of grass,
Hedgehog, breathing very heavily as he hunts for his insect
dinner.

Fox is slyly creeping through the tall grass,
Hunting for his dinner, a mouse or two will do,
Creeping, with his long bushy tail dragging along behind,
Licking his lips and cleaning his mouth ready for the taste of a
mouse.

Stephen Allen (11).

The Strange Crayfish

It glides through the water
By the muddy banks
And peeps into nooks and corners.
It watches all the others,
All very hard at work
Cutting down the reeds
To make some pale green toy.
But now what is this coming
Winding round the reed?
It has no fins to help it swim
But crawls quite fast
Through the wild water Jungle.
It has one pair of long sharp needles
Attached to its head.
Its eyes do frighten me
For they gleam, a bright, bright green.
I look once and then again.
I could not tell for sure
What that strange creature was
Crawling through the reeds.

Sarah Daykin (9).

The Worm

You feel the wriggle,
The twist and the turn,
The leathery skin,
Very dry from hard work,
You don't know where it lives,
And where it goes
On its way, wriggling about,
You pick it up and it seems
To come longer.

It's red and brown,
And seems to have two heads,
And seems to have two tails,
It lives in soil,
Beneath the plants and grass,
It seems to be everywhere you go,
I picked one up and it wriggled about,
It can be big and fat,
It can be small and thin.

Graham Banks (9).

The Ladybird

The ladybird is round and small,
Sometimes you see her on the wall.
Each Ladybird is a nice bright red,
With little black spots all over her head.

She walks through all the pastures green,
She is so small she can't be seen.
Then she climbs up fence and wall,
And up the oak tree very tall.

Then home she creeps back through the grass,
She is so lonely with no one to pass.
When home she comes from a tiring day
She has come a long, long way.

Allan Foster (11).

The Cat

As the cat walks in the dark
Its eyes gleam.
It purrs, it growls and scratches you
With its claws.
It sleeps on your knee sometimes.
Our cat sleeps on my bed.
I like it.

Diane Crisp (8).

The Dairy Cat

The dairy cat
Is ever so fat.
It eats and plays
But never a word says.
The Dairy cat can catch a rat,
That is why she's ever so fat!

Peter Chevins (8).

The Cat

Warming herself by the fire
Peacefully sleeps the cat.
Doesn't she look pretty,
Warming herself on the mat?

But look at her, now it is dark,
The very dead of night,
Quietly slinking along,
Her green eyes gleaming bright.

Carolyn Weatherald (10).

Sheba

Sheba is a cat with huge yellow eyes,
Yellow as the golden moon,
Her coat is as white as driven snow,
And her purring is like a cradle tune.

In winter she sits by the blazing fire,
Preening her soft white fur,
And when you stroke her gently, tenderly,
She will sweetly purr.

And when the Spring buds gently burst,
She plays gaily under the bed,
And when she longs for a long quiet rest,
She lies by the fire with her paws round her head.

In summer when the flowers bloom,
She sits amid the daisies bright,
And even when the sun sinks to rest,
She gently purrs on through the night.

But when the Autumn gales blow,
No better hound could God send,
For there she lies on the doormat brown,
Guarding our house to the end.

Catherine Brisbane (11).

9: STORMY WEATHER

THIS group of verses embraces the great variety of rain, wind and storm that has to be endured in our climate.

Mist is a common feature here, in the hills of this north country. Sometimes, indeed, it is the brief portent of a long, fine summer's day, but very often it covers the landscape with its grey shroud from morning to night, somehow, indefinably, affecting us all with its gloom, until at last it brings the rain.

Rain falls in so many ways, sometimes so gently that indeed we feel its blessing. Sometimes, driving in the wind, it beats on our windows in the darkness of the night, or it comes in such a heavy downpour that roads and fields are flooded. In the poems we see all this. Rain became of special interest to the children after we had decided to begin keeping rainfall records. We had previously recorded temperature, wind direction and so on, but for this project to be of value, and to establish a recognition that accuracy was vital, more demands would be made on the children's time. Nevertheless, this was soon understood, and during my last eight years at Askrigg rainfall was measured daily on a rota system, 365 days of the year. There was always a group of children of between eight and eleven who took it in turns, day by day, at week-ends, during holidays, on Christmas Day, to go to school and measure the rain that had accumulated in the gauge in the garden. Parents and old pupils co-operated wonderfully in this project, too, when necessary: if ever a child, whose turn it was, suddenly fell ill on a day when we were not at school, it was always quickly arranged for someone to step into the breach. The children were learning that truth was essential to science.

High winds always have an effect on children, and in these poems we feel the biting wind of winter, hear the rattling wind of autumn and are buffeted by the strong and teasing blasts of March. There are the winds that howl, that moan, that whistle, that whisper, that sing.

Thunder, of which most children are at first apprehensive, always aroused excitement, so I tried both to establish a proper respect for lightning and to put it in perspective. If a storm came on we always took time to consider it while it was happening. We would steadily count the seconds after the flash and calculate the distance, using the opportunity to compare the speeds of light and sound, until presently the sky's darkness lifted and at last we saw the rainbow.

Dark, wet and eerie,
The night is cold and rainy,
A wind is blowing.

Timothy Hill (11).

The Wind

Away on the hill tops the trees blow.
It is a cold, cold day.
The grass dances in the wind.
The birds shiver in the wind.
The clothes on the line blow.
The sky is grey, grey as snow.
It bows summer out and autumn in.

The leaves they blow away, away,
Into the wind on a windy day.
The doors they blow and bang and clatter,
The dustbin lids blow from their place,
Your hats fly into the air,
The wind carries them far away.
Your dresses blow up and up,
Paper blows on a windy day.

Lesley Allen (9).

The Wind

Wind a-whirling,
Leaves a-swirling,
All around,
To the ground.

The West wind brings rain,
Pitter patter on your window pane.
The North wind brings the cold,
And your cap you have to hold.

North wind freezes the pond,
You see snow on hills beyond.
Wind a-whirling,
Trees a-stirring.

North wind is wild,
And wakes a child
From his bed,
His sleepy head.

Kenneth Horner (11).

The Wind comes Howling

The wind comes howling through
The crack under the doorway
And comes through the keyhole.
I would rather be near the fire
Than outside in the rain.
Makes me think of ghosts
Prowling round the house.

Greta Kirkbride (11).

Storm on the hill tops
Dark thunder clouds threatening,
Fierce lightning flashes.

Christine Holdsworth (11).

A Storm

The distant sound of thunder,
Over the plains of the countryside,
Like a lion roaring
You can hear it.
Then flashes like a dragon's fire
Loom out in the dark.

Andrew Corney (10).

The Storm

The thunder smashes
The lightning flashes
But we are safe in school.
Then we look out
And let out a shout,
The field is just like a swimming pool.
The floods are rising
It's quite surprising
How quickly it should rise.
Cars are stuck
They have run out of luck,
As the rain pours from the skies.
The rain is stopping,
Mother's going shopping.
The clouds have gone away.
The sun comes out,
Without any doubt,
We've had a storm today.

Michael Gaskell (11).

The Rainbow

The rainbow is the prettiest thing,
It bends like a bridge,
It has a lot of colours,
Like red, green, yellow and mauve,
Some times it reflects,
And makes the prettiest pattern,
Then it fades away;
Three cheers for another day.

Margaret Pedley (9).

10: DAYS OF OLD

CHILDREN can become deeply interested in history, in its many forms, and will often go to a great deal of trouble, by the age of ten or eleven, to seek out authentic information and pictures to include in their work. It is not only the wealth of stories that are our heritage, but aspects of social and local history that can stir them deeply. The village, the houses, the church, the school, the shops, the fields, abandoned lead mines, old mills, old roads, and paths and railways are all fruitful subjects for study.

Within a short distance of Askrigg there are, for example, the site of prehistoric lake dwellings, Iron Age remains, a Roman fort and a fifteenth century crenellated farm house. Within a mile there had once been, for a few years, a Cistercian abbey where the monks had failed in the twelfth century to overcome the climatic rigours of Upper Wensleydale, and had travelled eastward, a few miles lower down the river valley, to try again and to succeed. There is Bolton Castle, too, the last remaining English stronghold to have sheltered the captive Mary, Queen of Scots, on her long, unhappy journey to her execution. The list could be continued.

The poems included here are sufficient to show the feeling for atmosphere and the imagination of the children, and one poem happily reflects the influence of Kipling.

The Empty Station

Woo, woo, chuff, chuff,
The trains say,
Puff, chuff, woo.
Now I think there's a train.
It puffs in the sky.
But the trains are scrap,
So is the track,
And they will never come back.
The station is ghostly
But I think it's mostly
The shadow of the people,
That walk by the track.
I wish the trains
Would come back.

Simon Bell (9).

Lost Forever

Once up on a hill,
On the grass there lay a muddy path,
But it also has been trampled on too many times.
It is now just a bit of clear grass waiting to be eaten.
The farmer is sometimes hopping mad when people do not take
To the path.
But they say that there is no path,
So he turns his nose up and disappears.
When visitors come the same thing happens,
So that everywhere that people tread,
There will be more paths Lost Forever.

Paul Allen (11).

The Old Mill

The old doors squeak,
And the floor boards creak,
The rats are shuffling behind the walls.
Broken glass on the floor,
Rusty hinges on the door,
On the roof are great, big stones,
Under the wheel squeaks and groans,
Broken bottles down below,
Cobwebs blowing to and fro.

Clinton Crisp (10).

Ripon Cathedral

Pillars stately, strong and tall,
Carvings of faces in each wall,
Altar, candles, cloth and all,
And people who follow Jesus's call.

The font is standing by the door,
And fossils lie in the Choir floor.
The statues come to life once more,
Of early Saints who lived before.

The glory of the Crypt below,
Built by Saint Wilfrid long ago,
Open unto friend, not foe,
The Ancient Christian faith to show.

Their joyful hymns the Choir sing,
Clear and sweet to the roof they ring,
Song rising up on lightest wing,
Joy in praising our Heavenly King.

Katie Abraham and Ruth Adinall (11).

Wensleydale

Can you see the shining river,
Winding through the dale,
That has wound as it does to-day,
Since the making of hill and vale?

Can you see the Roman road,
Steep and high, then low?
That is where the Romans marched,
Many years ago.

Can you see the castle grey,
Standing fine and bold?
Mary of Scotland was confined
Inside those walls so cold.

Catherine Brisbane (11).

11: AUTUMN

WHEN summer holidays were over at the end of August, the school assumed a changed appearance. Last term's stalwarts had gone, and their going was very noticeable, but the gap so suddenly created was always quickly bridged. The new challenge encouraged, and indeed enabled, their successors to grow to fill it. These younger children who had moved to the top would attain a surprising maturity by the time that another year had passed, as children in small country schools do. Everybody had made an upward move, and eagerness was in the air.

The onset of autumn was soon apparent. It was not so much that the year was drawing to its close, as that the most spectacular of all the seasons was beginning, and it always had its appeal to children. It aroused their instinct for gathering and collecting, and from the profusion of seeds and fruits some would be garnered as specimens for the nature table and displayed and studied in school. In the garden there were potatoes to be lifted and beetroot to be taken up. There were the herbaceous plants of summer to be cut down, and wilting nasturtiums to be removed. All had to be tidied before the onset of winter made such outdoor activity impossible.

In the mornings the migrant birds were congregating reflectively on the telephone wires, and spiders' webs on gates and trees glistened in the early sunlight. Already frosts were bringing the first crispness to the yellowing leaves that in a short time would be whirling in the wind. In the years when the rainfall had been lighter and the sun more generous, the glorious riot of autumn colour in the wood nearby became an even more magnificent sight; but soon the mists would roll along, and the days would come in November when we knew that the last of the summer migrants had gone, and the hedgehogs and the squirrels were asleep. There was much to be seen and heard in autumn, and much of it has been captured and described in these poems.

Autumn

Autumn is the loveliest time of the year.
All the summer crops are gathered in
Ready for the winter.
Leaves are coloured by the sun,
Orange, yellow, brown and green.
Squirrels prepare their winter stock
Under trees and behind rock.
Leaves are falling faster now,
Winter's on its way.

Alastair Dinsdale (10).

Autumn

Autumn has come at last,
All the leaves are falling fast,
All the birds are going away,
Only the robin wants to stay.

The bracken now is yellow and red,
And earlier we go to bed.
The leaves are falling
And the owl is calling.

Ella Metcalfe (10).

Autumn

Yellow the leaves,
Yellow the sheaves,
Rosy the berries,
Bare are the trees.

The fog is falling,
The rain is pouring,
The stream is full,
The sky looks dull.

Will Pedley (10).

Autumn has come

Autumn has come,
And Summer has gone,
And the fruits are growing upon
The trees that are turning yellow,
The wind is blowing like a bellow.

The leaves turn orange, yellow and red,
Then they fall upon your head,
And they seem to make a bed
For little animals cold and red
With the wind and snow.

When the leaves have blown away,
The trees are bare for many a day,
The winter has come,
And Autumn has gone,
And the green, green grass is snowed upon.

Valerie Cockerill (10).

Autumn

In the Autumn season
Nuts grow and leaves fall;
Down the lane, across the field,
And on the river bank
A rich carpet of Gold, Red and Yellow is spread.
Hedgehogs fatten and Squirrels hide
Their hoards of nuts,
While the graceful swallow
Flies to sunny countries.
The flies and gnats in squadrons fly
While robins hunt for berries.
Beautiful Toadstools gather in clusters
By the tree trunks
And the spiky Horse Chestnut
Drops from its socket.

Richard Brisbane (10).

October Morning

This morning was like having a blanket of mist and fog put over you.
You could not see the sun at all.
Last night you could not see where you were going, at all.
Our school bus had to have fog lights.
You could not see the bright leaves in the sunshine.

Bruce Fawcett (9).

An October Morning

On an October morning
The dew and the frost lie on the ground,
And the spider's web sparkles
After the dew has settled on it.
And the birds are sitting on the wire, ready to fly away,
And the yellow, orange and rust leaves
Are floating down from the trees.
The robins are getting redder breasts,
And the fruits are ready for picking.

Stephen Porter (10).

Falling Leaves

As I was walking in the wood
I saw the leaves had fallen.
The day before the leaves were red,
Yellow, green and golden.

Neil Haw (9).

November Days

Fogs and dark days come with November,
Not snows and Christmas, like in December,
Just dark morning and night,
But we can sit in the jolly fire-light.

Out in the fog we can't see our way,
And my torch only lets out a very small ray,
Sometimes we have some snow,
The wind does loudly blow.

The squirrel and hedgehog are asleep,
And some of the bulbs begin to peep,
The frosts are very bad,
And the trees in white are clad.

Vivian Burton (10).

12: AT SCHOOL

IN THESE poems the children picture themselves at play, and, because dinner is such a highly important part of their day, there is one about that, too. Meals were always served in what we liked to think of as our hall, in reality a large, spare classroom which somewhat kaleidoscopically would change its pattern many times a day. It would begin with the children assembled for morning prayers, and at break they would be drinking their milk there. At other times there would be a maze of benches, stools, mats and horizontal bars arranged for physical education on rainy days; a spread of instruments for music — chime bars and glockenspiel, tambourines and triangles; displays of attractive new books in their colourful jackets; bright paint and paste and paper for art and craft; tawny, orange octagonal tables laid for dinner.

School dinners were cooked in the adjoining kitchen, and were unfailingly attractive in appearance, as well as being wholesome and well balanced. We never rushed the meal, so that the youngest of children with the tiniest of appetites always had time to finish without being hurried. There was time to talk, too, and the range of conversation was wide and the topics often surprising—no small contribution to the fluency which we strove to make a firm basis of our work. Throughout the years the majority of children looked forward to the dinners and enjoyed them immensely. I have sometimes thought with what pleasure such meals would have been received when compulsory education began a hundred years ago. No one at all went home for the midday meal, so there was no part of the playtime that any child had to miss, and this gave us a corporate life throughout the day.

The school is now a century old, and has seen many changes. In the playground the sound of the voices, the endless chatter, the merry laughter, the squeals, the cries of glee, the ferocious shouts, the sudden burst of temper, the distressed sobs that, with a little comforting, so quickly change to smiles, will always be the same.

The Playground

The playground is lonely in the morning,
Then the children come shouting in.
Soon the football begins.
"Hooray!" shouts somebody "We've scored."
Suddenly the whistle is blown,
The playground is left to itself.
The children are busy singing hymns.
Then doing decimal sums.
Soon all come out except poor Alan.
He has put his Decimal point in the wrong place.
The little ones are playing tig,
The big ones are playing football again.
Big boys, little boys and middle sized too,
All busy playing happily away.

Frank Fawcett (10).

The Playground

The patter of the children's feet
And echo of the voices,
But not all the time is there joy,
For some fall on their faces.

In the evening all is dim,
And nothing to be seen,
For every child is in bed
Until the night has been.

But sometimes things are noisy,
For everybody's at play,
And everybody's happy
Until the end of the day.

Andrew Brisbane (11).

Reading

To the book corner Tom goes,
He can read, as he knows.
He picks up a book
Called Peter Pan and Captain Hook.
He goes back to his chair,
Sits down and reads there.
Page after page, he reads on,
Then he says Where has Peter gone?
Then he says I've finished my book for to-day,
Now I will put it back, and go to play.

Michael Gaskell (9).

In the Playground

In the playground children play.
They play so gay,
They jump and run
And have lots of fun.

Some children play football
But not all.
When the whistle goes
The children come in and warm their toes.

Bernard Percival (11).

The Playground

The playground is silent as night,
But when playtime comes
The pattering of feet and shouting drowns the silence.
Everybody is happy and gay,
Especially when it's time to play.
Sometimes an unlucky person falls,
That brings the gayness out of him.
In a few minutes time he is happy and gay again.
The football is kicked all round the yard,
There is no rush to get it when it goes over the wall.
Sometimes there is a crash and a tinkle,
Everybody knows that a window has been broken.
All of a sudden a whistle goes,
The yard is then silent again.

William Banks (11).

Dinner-time

Potatoes, Gravy, cabbage and meat,
Makes a most delightful treat,
Strawberries, Jelly and Ice Cream,
Are things you would never dream.
Fifty people go into the room,
Because now it's twelve noon.
After dinner they go to play,
They can't wait for dinner next day.

Next day there's Yorkshire Pudding to eat,
With Potatoes and roast meat.
Now it's time to serve.
These are things we did not deserve.
It's time to say grace,
And they all jump up out of their place.
Now it's time to go out and play,
They can't wait for dinner next day.

Colin Teasdale (11).

13: CHRISTMAS

CHRISTMAS is the exciting climax of the year in school, and these verses capture the feeling of the fun of parties and games, the hanging up of stockings and the delight in anticipation of presents to come, the glowing fires, the carols and the winter cold; and at the heart of it all, the Christmas story itself.

Weeks beforehand, preparations began. Gaily coloured decorations, cards and calendars were made, and, as the time approached, the rooms were adorned with paper chains and silver stars, lanterns and mobiles of shepherds and angels and Father Christmas. Pastes and papers, paints and brushes, needles and scissors were in feverish use. There were careful rehearsals of bible readings and music for the carol service, which took place in the parish church, dedicated to Saint Oswald, so beloved by our northern forefathers, and parents and friends joined us here.

Sometimes, before the holiday, we went to an old people's home and to a local hospital to entertain the patients. They always enjoyed the children's singing, and liked to join in old, familiar carols and hymns, which must have recalled for them other, distant days. Occasionally there would be time for a chat, and the sympathetic bond between the old and the very young was always striking.

About ten days before the holiday the Christmas tree appeared, and was hoisted and made fast in its appointed place by the many eager hands waiting excitedly to decorate it. The lovely glass baubles, many of which had long been treasured in our homes were carefully removed from their crumpled tissue paper and hung about the branches. Finally, it only remained for me to place the silver star on top, and the tree dominated the scene.

Near the end of term came the Christmas dinner, graciously served at the gaily coloured tables with their gleaming, stainless steel dishes, and always received and eaten with great enthusiasm. Roast pork, with all its adjuncts, tenderly cooked, was followed by plum pudding, made from an old and well-tried recipe; and little pots, full of bright sprigs of holly, adorned the tables. The occasion provided an opportunity for the head boy to make a speech.

Finally came the Christmas party, which by a little planning with the bus operators and parents we were always able to have when afternoon school was over, a popular custom. There really was a party atmosphere when the old, traditional games could be played in the warmth and glow of artificial light. The clear and strong young voices never seemed to tire, however long the lines might be for "A-hunting we will go", or however many children must have their due turn at

"Nuts in May". Best clothes were always worn and boys would often have a newly knitted pullover. There were elaborate paper hats, too, designed and made by their wearers specially for the occasion. The party began with an abundant tea, with jellies and trifles, sandwiches and cakes, largely provided by mothers, and it ended with the distribution of simple presents. This was a day when every member of the school staff, whatever their normal duties, would be there to help and to take pleasure in the helping. The caretaker, the cook, the secretary, the meals helpers, the vicar, who was also the chairman of the managers, would all be there with the teachers, hard at work, and all enormously enjoying the fun.

While writing this I have come across a small boy's pencilled couplet that I had folded away with a Christmas party programme twenty years ago. Here is expressed the true joy of anticipation:

"Hooray! It's party day to-day,
And when it's time we'll play and play".

And the Christmas party was one of the events that usually measured up to what was expected of it.

As one goes through life and sees that Christmas becomes more and more secular in its manner of celebration, its meaning so often lost, we can be glad that there is perhaps no better place than in our primary schools for keeping alive in children's minds the birth of the Christ child, and its significance for us. The stories of the nativity are heard afresh each year; and hymns and carols, old and new, are sung again with the love, the enthusiasm and the cheerful, willing effort of childhood that we need to hold on to, for here are the foundations of our hopes for the future.

Christmas

On the eve of Christmas day
Jesus was born in a manger of hay,
While the three wise men
Came to see Jesus in Bethlehem.

The wise men were clad in fur,
Some brought incense and some brought myrrh.
That is why we always are gay
On the morning of Christmas day.

Robert Trotter (10).

Mary

Mary had a little son,
It was her holy one.
Three Wise Men came to see him,
Gifts they all did bring him.

An angel went to the shepherds,
To tell them and their flocks and herds,
If they were able,
To go and see him in a stable.

In his boyhood,
He was good.
He was a teacher,
And a preacher.

James Cooper (9).

Christmas

One day there was a boy,
And for Christmas he got a toy.
It was an aeroplane big and new,
It was a lovely one painted blue.

Round and round he flew it all day,
And he was happy and very gay,
Until the end of the day came,
And he had finished his little game.

Paul Metcalfe (10).

The Christmas Birth

One day, a long time ago,
Joseph and Mary trudged through the snow,
They went to live in Bethlehem.
To find a house they were not able,
All they could get was a stable.

Mary then had a baby,
An angel came and said 'Maybe
We will call your son Jesus'.
A huge star came and kept them from danger,
As the baby lay in a manger.

Late came the shepherds,
Led by a star,
Leaving their herds,
O'er the hills from afar.

Along came the wise men,
Carrying staffs made of pines,
Brought along with them
Gold, Frankincense and Myrrh, for signs.

Maureen Porter (10).

The Snow

The snow did fall, very light,
Deeper and deeper, all through the night.
Dark and dreary was the morn,
That was the time when Christ was born.

Men feed the sheep near the lake,
While we in the house eat wine and cake.
Birds look for tiny scraps of crumb,
Fast asleep are the bees with their hum.

Anne Hindle (10).

The Wise Men

By the light of the stars
Wise men came from the east,
They came on camels and on horses.
The wise men were in their golden robes,
And they were carrying gold, myrrh and frankincense.

The robes were as bright as a star,
And they shone like diamonds,
They shone so brightly that it would blind you,
They were following a star that shone in the west.

The star shone right over Bethlehem,
It was right over a stable,
And in that stable there were some oxen.
In a cradle Jesus lay,
And Mary and Joseph were by his side.

Robert Fawcett (10).

Jesus's Bed

Jesus in a manger lay,
He had a soft bed of hay,
It was so soft and neat,
And he had presents at his feet.

Even shepherds came to praise
And said, 'Live happy all thy days'.
Then came three kings and saw him there,
In a stable cold and bare.

'In the East we saw your star,
And we travelled from afar.
Why art thou born in this stall
Thou should have been born in a hall'.

Olwyn Teasdale (10).

Christmas

It was on a night of December,
The night that we remember,
The night that Jesus was born,
Early in the morn.

In a stable he did lie,
He did laugh and he did cry.
From the east three kings came,
Through mountain, moor and lane.

It happened on a cold, cold night,
The stars were very, very bright.
That night bells did ring,
Angels did sing.

Angels did sing praises to the king
Praises to the king,
Then the shepherds heard the news,
When they got there they took off their shoes.

Children came to see the Babe
Where in a manger he was laid.
He was little and weak,
Three kings for him did seek.

Kenneth Horner (10).

On Christmas Eve

It was a cold and frosty night
And the wind howled.
The snow came heavily down,
The fire was hot and bright.

The sky was dark,
The stars were bright,
And now the fire was burning low,
And carol singers sang to us
The carols that we know.

Julie Sharples (10).